By the same author:

Don Marcelino's Daughter

Unequal Thirds

KYRIE

Tim Cunningham

A WHITE HOUSE POETRY BOOK

Revival Press
Limerick - Ireland

Copyright © Tim Cunningham 20

First published
Revival Pre
Morav
Glenmore Aven
Roxboro Ro;
Limeri
Irelar

www.revivalpress.

In association with t
White House Poe

www.myspace.com/thewhitehousepoe

Book design: Kelly Richards Printing, Limeric
Cover design: Aisling Burk
Cover image: Eamonn McCarth
Printed and bound by: GraphyCems, Spai
Author photograph: Eamonn Mc Carth

The author can be contacted for readings, interviews etc at revivalpress@eircom.n(

Project editor: Dominic Taylc

ISBN 978-0-9554722-4-

A CIP catalogue record for this book is available from The British Librar

Contents

for Carolyn

THE GARDEN OF EDEN

The Garden of Eden had a nettle patch,
Dockleaf bandages, hosts of white-haired
Dandelions, buttercup doubloons, daisies
Periscoping through a cobbled yard.

The tap was by a wooden gate. Fetching
Water in July was like stealing the sun;
On frosty nights, I carried in a slice
Of moon, a bucketful of stars.

The garden had no snake, no tree, no apples.
And still a voice called down behind a cloud,
Thundered its expulsion writ, decreed
Bread must be earned ' by the sweat of your brow'.

My garden did exist; I have the sepia proof
Captured by a Brownie box camera:
The serried smiles of family ghosts
Framed against a blazing wall of ivy.

Home on holiday, I pass the barred
And bolted gate. And there he is,
All cap, tattoos and navy uniform,
That flaming angel with a sword.

MISSION WEEK

They turned up once a year like Duffy's
Circus, the two Redemptorists:
One with blowlamp tongue stripping
Paint from the city's peeling soul,

The other's brushes dipped in tins
Of beatific light. Keen
As Pentecostal wind, they stormed
The pulpit steps in black birettas

And soutanes, rosaries dangling
From their belts like rope ladders
To heaven. One stoked embers of fear,
Made words glow like burning coals

Indelibly searing his picture
Of hell and fanning its flames
With eternity's huge bellows.
The other squeezed words to diamonds:

Jewels in the Virgin's tiara,
A celestial treasure hoard.
Their leaving was the folding of tents.
Amen to trapeze, strong man,

The chair and whip in the Daniel cage.
Back then to the tip-toe, soot-soft
Words of the curate at St. Michael's:
His index finger writing on sand

The secrets of heaven and hell,
His passport stamped at both borders.

PANIS ANGELICUS

A limestone steeple was the tallest oak
And the church bell sang
Like a metal bird that August morning:
The bride's dress white as altar linen,
The sun's rays sanctified
By stained glass windows,
The tenor in black soutane trilling
'*Panis Angelicus*' from the organ loft,
Clear as a bird in the hawthorn.
A lark in search of lyrics for her song
Would have to look no further.

HER PURE SOPRANO

They spoke of her in whispers on the street
      Just like the slanted way they might have talked
About that swollen girl in Nazareth
      If some old Joe had not agreed to walk
With her on other streets and save her shame
By gifting her the shelter of his name.

Whispering had never been her style
      But consonants of stone, helium vowels.
Not for her the sly, behind-back tale,
      The serpent hissing of the kiss-and-tell.
Pitched between earth and eternity,
Her clarion words rang out in major keys.

Clustered in the organ loft, the choir
      Were blackbirds singing from the tallest branch.
Faith honeyed their fervent repertoire,
      Especially her pure soprano chanting
The Latin praises of that mother's child
Tender as vernacular lullabies.

THE WATERCOLOUR MADONNA

Ethereal in blue and white,
The watercolour Madonna
Took pride of place
In the window:

Blue eyes, blue mantle,
Blue sash tied
About her waist,
The bluest of skies;

White dress, white veil,
White halo, white roses
Scattered at her
Bare, white feet.

But the sun has it in
For watercolours,
Melts white like snow,
Steals back light,

Especially the blue.
Its laser rays
Softened, bleached,
Imperceptibly erased

The mantle and sash,
The radiant eyes,
The sky we used
To call celestial.

FAST LATIN

Father Pat lived life in the fast lane,
Saying weekday mass (minus sermon
Or homily) in fifteen minutes flat.

He hit the introit like a sprinter
Rocketing from his starting blocks,
Tongue spiked for the cinder track

Of Latinate vowels, clipped consonants.
Offertory, sanctus, consecration, Agnus Dei
Accelerated with his record times

As he breasted, too soon, the tape stretched taut
Across the threshold of eternity.
The funeral bell almost apologised.

The mourners reminisced, agreed on speed:
That one so slow to judge, quick to compassion,
Was guaranteed his place among the medals.

CATHEDRALS

Alone in the cathedral, I knelt
As if waiting for benediction.
An odd place to arrange to meet
But we both knew it well
And it was shelter from the showers.
The minutes mounted up. No sign.
Late became a definite no-show.
I genuflected towards the tabernacle,
Crept quietly away, a cathedral mouse,
Blessed myself with holy water.

Alone along the riverbank, I walked
The gravelled aisle, smelling evening's incense
And lilac blossoming in shrines of broken walls.
A blackbird in the thorn bush intoned vespers.
Hedgerows wore the vestments of the day.
Light splintered through a stained-glass sky
As haws flickered their sanctuary lamps,
Acolytes touched their tapers to the stars,
The elevated moon shone like a host.
And still no bell to promise benediction.

LILIES OF THE FIELD

Not a Solomon in sight.
Arrayed in working clothes
For weekday mass, they kneel,
Scattered like sturdy seed,
Their rough hands weathered
With toil, grained with spinning;
Foreheads furrowed, harrowed
With the passing years
Of care that will not pass,
With secrets whispered to the feet
Of plaster saints, and hopes
Pinned on penny candles
Flickering at the shrine
Of the Madonna. And still
They kneel and keep the faith,
Their white heads bent in reverence
Like the lilies of the field.
Outside, sparrows and starlings
That neither sow nor reap
Score telegraph wires,
And the blackbird's song
Is pitched too high for elegy.

MYSTERY TOURS

They blossomed with the daffodils,
Those seasonal mystery tours.
And she blossomed in her window seat:
Shoes polished, coat brushed,
Ticket safe inside her purse

As the single-decker bolted
From the station, snapped the city's
Corset, the snort of salt and mountain
Air already in its lungs.
Hedges and fields bumped past on rutted

Roads with their display of blackthorn,
Granite rocks, a piebald with her
Painted foal. They stopped at towns
And landmarks that put pictures
To familiar names. Then back on board,

Engine labouring the slopes
Or helter-skeltering towards the sea.
Sunsets stowed back with them, framed
In rear-view mirrors. And all too soon
The spilling like Smarties from the bus.

They laughed their way down side streets,
Fluttered like moths to the window
Of each home. A slice of sleep and then
The bell for Sunday mass, the standing
For the gospel's **A** to **Z**.

The first snowdrops were out the day
The ambulance arrived, the day
She took those few steps from the door:
Shoes polished, coat brushed, Murillo's
Madonna safe inside her purse.

ALTAR

Light conspires with liturgy,
Floods the high altar for Sunday mass.
The tongues of six white candles speak
Of tables set for high supper.
The priest, successor to Mechisedech,
Breaks bread, sips consecrated wine,
Kisses the altar stone, takes centre stage
In the hypnotic pageantry
Of chalice, chasuble, incense, flowers.
An orchestra conducted by the sun.

Is it a trick of the light
That sees the Judas spectre at the feast?
The Isaac child with kindling on his back
Toiling sanctuary steps,
Trailblazing the sharp road to Golgotha?
The flash of sacrificial knives?
Blood seeps from relics in the altar stone,
And everywhere the hammering of nails.
Extinguished candles whisper 'mizbeah':
'Altar', 'a place of slaughter'.

SIDE ALTAR

Side altars are discreet,
Prefer the shield of shadow
To liturgical pomp

As if the quiet priest
Chooses a kitchen snack
Against five-star hotels.

No mitres here, no gold
And diamond-studded crozier.
Only the shepherd's staff.

The two candle award
Illuminates just size.
For quality, six

Candles every time.
Perhaps, through infra-reds
Of faith, we might observe

No less a radiance,
No less a feast of light,
And thrill to some archangel's

Golden trumpet, the golden
Notes of seraphim's
Schola cantorum.

Even with 'a glass
Through which we see darkly'
Or otherwise, the kindling

Burns as fiercely, the nails
Ring just as cruel,
The hammering as loud.

Here, no less a sacrifice.
The tears are just as real
Along this Via Dolorosa.

TABERNACLE

It was bold, this house of gold,
Its golden door on fire, alive,
Dead centre on the high altar,

Regal, expecting the homage of bent
Knees. The sanctuary lamp flickered
Saying God was in.

They moved Him to a side altar.
I see their point, a changing
Liturgy for changing times,

Diluted like whiskey on the rocks,
An accessible deity discreet about
His thunderclap and lightning bolt,

A guy-next-door god
Who can share a pint
And chat about the football scores.

But some old codgers moan,
Imagine the whiz kids
Have taken over the manor,

Cobbled together
A granny-annexe-bathchair-god
To wheel out on occasion.

SACRISTY

'How closely do you look?
How much exactly do you see?'
We took up his challenge
To lazy youth, scanned
The sacristy with CCTV eyes
(Long before CCTVs),
A sixty second scrutiny
And then eyes closed, no cheating.

I think that I was right about the clock,
Not just about the time, a Smith,
And right about the bunch of keys,
The colours of the ceiling, walls,
The missal on the table,
The brass collection plate, lost glove.
Wrong about the maniple,
The raincoat (Aquascutum) on the hook.

Now I can recall filling glass cruets,
Burning charcoal for the thurible,
Checking that vestments were the colour of the day,
Flicking switches for altar and aisles,
Meeting James Cagney ('You dirty rat!')
Shovelling through the records for his roots,
The scratch of rats like 'Exorcist' extras,
Droppings on a chasuble in the drawer.

Most clearly, I still see the parish clerk
With candle grease pearling his black soutane,
Explaining headlines from a wider world
(The morning paper spread like Caesar's map),
Biting his nails with porcelain teeth,
The only thing about him that was false.
And I barely remember the visiting priest
Who forgot why his hands were anointed.

MORTUARY

This was the room of temporary rest
Between evening's procession to the chapel
(Those soft vowels of condolence, each handshake
A unique grip, the half familiar faces –
Tangents to the circle of his life)
And morning's mass for which he can't be late.

Deposited like left luggage, his varnished
Coffin perched on two tall trestles,
The brass handles and silver plaque hoarding
Remnants of the light. Above him, the stone
Ceiling; beside him, walls of grey concrete;
Below him, a cold geometry of tiles.

The room of bed without breakfast is changed,
Transformed into a mundane storage space
For Lalor's beeswax candles, sanctuary oil,
A tarnished thurible, carbolic soap,
Buckets, mops and, in the farthest corner,
A brush and pan for sweeping up the dust.

THE LEPERS' SQUINT

They call it The Lepers' Squint:
The hole in the cathedral's north wall,
In the Holy Spirit Chapel
Tucked away left of the organ pipes,
Where mediaeval lepers pressed
To peer in at the service,
Queued for the bread of heaven.

They call it the hole in the wall:
The cash dispenser centuries along the street,
Left of the blind musician
Where pigeons peck at crisp bags
Littering the city's north transept.
We congregate, press pin numbers,
Squinting in the sun.

SPANISH MARBLE

Samson could not topple these pillars,
This Spanish marble rooted in the centre aisle,
Atlas shoulders bearing the church ceiling.
Metaphors for polished power and beauty,
Their muscular aesthetic flexes, blends
Natural as oak in Cratloe Woods.

They stand alert, straight-backed sentinels,
Witnesses to liturgies of praise,
To nuptial vows and solemn requiems,
To life's alphas and omegas and that
Brief path stretching between. If they had leaves,
Those columns would give shelter from the storm.

And down the street, a restaurant with open
Doors and parquet floor, flowers fit for shrines,
Enormous discs of table tops hewn
From identical stone. We sit down
At these altars, find something sacramental
In the breaking of French bread.

THE GOLD ARCHANGEL

'of celestial armies prince'

'Paradise Lost', vi.44

The gold archangel towers
On the belltower of St. Michael's,
Body armour burnished in the sun,
Spear at Satan's reptile throat,
A view unchanged down Chapel Street,
A constant for each generation's eyes.

Inside the church's limestone walls,
The silent clash of sword on shield,
Combatants invited from highways
And parochial by-ways
Like beggars to a feast.
Kneeling in their bloodless battlefield,

Sons of Adam, hands calloused with toil,
Daughters burdened with supermarket bags,
Glimpse a beatific glow,
Hear choirs of cherubim and seraphim
Or catch the foul sulphuric stench
Rising from some Stygian lake.

Leaving, they spot the bird on Michael's head,
The pumped crow puffed up with delusion
Like the fabled wren that soared highest
But on the golden eagle's back,
Like that once bright archangel
Who 'trusted to have equalled the Most High.'

CRUCIFIX

Refurbishing the church,
    They refurbished the theology.
    Removing marble altar rails
Was lowering the drawbridge,
    Emptying the moat,
    A glasnost liturgy
Like bringing altars forward.

Celebrants came forward too
    And faced the congregation.
    Such contrast with the Byzantine priest
Receding to the hidden altar,
    Passing through the sanctuary's screen
    Of heavenly icons,
'Becoming an angel'.

Ditto tabernacles
    Changing address
    From high altar mansions
But domiciled in the same post code,
    Moved to a side altar annex
    And no less a Real Presence
Despite the 'welcome' mat.

Here in the centre aisle,
    The crucifix has disappeared.
    Instead, Christ hovering
Above a golden cross,
    Regal in His resurrection robes.
    Again, the desideratum
Of religion without nails.

THE STATIONS OF THE CROSS

They spin like chairoplanes,
These stations of the cross,

A dizzy carousel
Revolving at the per

Second per second
Speed of contemplation,

Filtering, sifting
Twenty four carat scenes:

Meeting the compassion
In His mother's eyes,

Simon of Cyrene
Helping with the load,

The tears of the Daughters
Of Jerusalem,

Veronica
Pushing through the crowd,

Elbowing her way
Like a paparazzo,

Rewarded with His likeness
Imprinted on her veil.

THE STATUE OF THE VIRGIN

Nightlights flicker on her shrine like stars:
The heavenly queen, first among statues,
Crowned in the beauty pageant of the soul.

Her dress and veil almost flutter, painted
In blue and white and immaculate light.
You can smell the stone roses at her feet.

She looks down from her pedestal, accepts
With grace the litanies of praise, the hymns
To Mary, Virgin Mother, Star of the Sea.

A likely apparition at some grotto,
Acquainted with the repertoire from school
Nativity play to intimate pietas,

She looks down at the children's daisy eyes
Opening towards the sun of bright tomorrows.
The woodland's bluebell floor invites their feet.

She looks down at the liver-spotted hands,
The white cane tapping on the centre aisle;
Reads on harrowed foreheads seasons of regret.

She looks down at the girl stanching tiny
Dams of tears, the girl whose secret was not
Whispered by an angel in her ear.

PIETA

To find the pieta, follow
The buzz and flight of flies, look for
The penny candle's flame warming
The coldest corner of the church.

A long road down from Bethlehem,
This chalk and plaster Christ lies draped
Again across his mother's lap,
His head again against her breast,

His body cold, the kind of cold
An ox's fervent breath can't reach.
Mothers understand pietas.
Most have their quiet depositions.

Some kneel, holding the memory
Of hands they led from crib to crib
Across the glistening Christmas snow.
One for certain that I know.

Flies were buzzing in the field
The day my friend, a mere unlucky
Thirteen years, collapsed at play and died,
The morning he was lifted up

Across the garden wall, the garden
That became his parents' own
Gethsemane, the wall that shaped
Itself to their pieta.

FONTS

In this city, Moses would not need
       To strike a rock. Anonymous, I ghost
       Inside the church out of the rain, and instinct
Dips my fingers in the limestone font.

More chiselled limestone in the baptistry
       And a latter-day John the Baptist pouring
       Water on a baby's head. It trickles,
Circles, silvers down the Jordan basin.

Leaving, a flash of sun snaps my reflection
       In the font. My fingerprints float on water.
       Outside, rain patters on the street's keyboard,
Touchtypes my name in Roman font.

PULPIT

The pulpit looms proud as a chariot
Strutting its peacock chest, its high
Dashboard sparkling with silver, burnished

With beaten gold. The preacher climbs the winding
Steps like a champion charioteer
At the Circus Maximus, eager for gates

To snap open, then the seven thundering
Laps, the lightning finish down
The straight. His armour is the chasuble,

His helmet, the three-finned biretta.
His text cuts deep as javelins.
His homily hurls its thunderbolts, competes

With Boadicea fixing swords to her axles,
With Elijah's fiery horses
Harnessed to a chariot of flame.

ORGAN

King of instruments,
The organ prowls its jungle gallery,
Shakes its Masai Mara mane,
Clears its Krakatoa throat.

Its sin is pride,
Preening itself,
Flicking a tail
At siesta flies.

Narcissus-like,
It catches its reflection
In the pool of polished boards.
So much to esteem:

The hand-carved console
Finished in light oak,
Periscope pipes,
Ivory draw-stops, pistons,

Crescendo pedals,
The Perspex roll-top
Inviting admiration
While shielding a litany of parts.

Forgivable vanity
When keys are touched
Unlocking the 'Te Deum'
Or 'Jesu, Joy of Man's Desiring'.

Its lungs are pentecostal.
And what can be as pure
As an instrument
Born to praise?

A SIDE-AISLE SEAT

Immaculate in polished boots,
Pressed uniform, nervous cane
Adjusting his peaked cap,
The officer half smiled, rattled
Off the pep-talk learned by heart,
Shuffled at the bits best left
Unsaid, addressed the men as 'chaps'.

Chaps who thought only of love
To see them through the war.
And one who sat (the hourglass sand
Whipping across his face) silent
As if home at Sunday mass
Daydreaming through the sermon
('Dearly beloved . . .') beside her

In their favourite side-aisle seat.
She would be wearing summer shoes,
The cotton dress he bought at Todds
For her nineteenth birthday,
The Bergman 'Casablanca' hat,
But black out of respect for church,
Not yet for mourning.

MISERICORDS

(St. Mary's Cathedral, Limerick)

Standing was the prayer posture
With arms outstretched
Like the crucified Christ.

Then the relaxed rubric
Allowing frail bodies
The support of staff and crutch.

Later, the *misericords*:
The merciful lips
Of clergy stalls

Propping their weary weight
Straight like saplings,
And the underside of seats

Offering woodcarvers
Playgrounds of oak,
Challenging their

Pious craft. The chiselling
Survives, cool and hard
As onyx, smooth as slate.

One shows the antelope:
Serrated horns
Picturing old

And new testaments,
Not a dilemma but twin
Powers warring against

Evil. Another illustrates
The lion and wyvern,
Love wrestling hate,

The resurrection symbol
Locked with anti-Christ.
Like a plump 'S',

The swan paddles, her
Martyr song
Blending with the choir.

An eagle soars high
Above cockatrice
And griffin in the bestiary,

Eyes fixed on the sun
And plunging three times in water
Reflecting baptism

And the Saviour who
Said, 'I carried
You on eagle wings and brought you

To myself.' Art and religion
Sit well together in dark
Stalls, stalls remembering

Their youth in Cratloe
Woods: birds welcome as light
In their branches, lovers'

Initials cut fervent
With initial love,
Acorns dropping their hint

Of future. In woods and cathedral,
Merciful oak dreams
Of religion without nails.

CONFESSIONAL

This is the laundry for the soul.
        Pop it in and the grime of sin
        Will wash away like shirt stains
On the cuffs and round the collar.

Contrition is the powder
        To restore it good as new,
        Not a spot deserving of
That purgatorial purge.

But this is still a box of shame,
        A bank where we deposit guilt;
        Pandora and Medusa
Have been seen here after dark.

This is a place of secrecy,
        A whispering gallery
        Where the priest is god's ventriloquist
Pronouncing absolution

Like the priest who heard my first
Confession, his smiling mouth
        Across the grid lifting with words
The weight of all my seven years

As if remembering the day
        He first opened the box, emerging
        Shiny as a coin pressed
Overnight in a raw potato.

TRESTLES

Easy to add 'Amen'
When the kind old priest assured us
That her race was won
And prayed attendant angels
To lead her
Onto heaven's podium.

Not so easy when he prayed for rest,
Knowing her preference for eternal zest.
But I took cheer
From her coffin's
High hurdle trestles
And the candle's Olympic flame.

PALL

For funerals, the light streams paler
Through stained-glass windows,
Transforms white marble to sarcophagi,
Alters altar linen to winding sheets.

Paler, yes, and cooler too.
The avenue of pillars loses heat,
Not a green leaf fluttering,
Not a migratory feather.

Heels clink on centre and side aisles
Like ice cubes in a glass.
Mourners come in silent waves;
Their black tide fills the seats.

And then the polished coffin
Shouldered in by relatives and friends,
Placed before the sanctuary gate,
Holy like a sacrifice, a bride.

Six tall black candles stand
Like sentinels, flicker
A hint of Viking lords
Pushed blazing out to sea,

Of pyres beside the Ganges
And ashes of the dead
Tossed on the sacred river
In hope of favourable rebirth.

The celebrant swings his thurible;
Incense purifies, drives away
Demons, pleases the gods,
Conceals the smell of death.

Water also purifies.
He sprinkles the coffin,
Blesses the boat as it embarks
Across the cavernous Styx.

The pall spreads its black
Membrane underneath the coffin,
Hides wooden trestles the way
Victorians concealed piano legs,

The way bats' wings unfold:
A shadow stitched with white borders,
A final magic carpet,
A low cloud of unknowing.

CHALICE

I think again of Viking raids,
The prows of longships raping the wild coast,
Then Harry's Heroes looting monasteries,
Gems too rich for God being perfect for his coffers.
The thud of axe and sword on skull and bone,
The dying screams still echo down

From illustrated textbook and classroom.
And pictures like the perfect Ardagh chalice,
Goblets fit for the King of kings,
Precious silver shaped to works of art,
Jewel-studded, lined with beaten gold,
Receptacles for far more precious blood,

Blood spilled back in Gethsemane
When that young Jew knelt down among the olives,
Saw his chalice and prayed for it to pass,
A prayer futile as asking His disciples
Not to sleep, to keep vigil.
'Will you not watch one hour with me?'

Housebound for those final years,
My grandmother's Gethsemane
Was the living room. Sitting
By the window, looking out
Across the green to Clare's far greener,
Restless, patchwork hills,

She watched the sun play peek-a-boo
Or sulk behind deep-bellied cloud,
Predicted weather ex-cathedra
But only when the mist had settled
Or dispersed by half past ten.
And never spoke about her shining grail,

The children flown like geese across the hills.
Never spoke about her chalice,
Not a hint except that afternoon.
Every day, I drink the memory
Of her sotto-voce vowels asking
Me, for just one hour, to stay.

CIBORIUM

Ciboria are squat, not tall and sleek,
More hall-of-mirror chalices
With low centres of gravity.

But also jewel-studded, lined
With beaten gold to hold a body
Once laid on golden straw.

A long queue forms up the centre aisle,
The congregation hungry
For the food of the soul.

The priest holds the ciborium,
Descends the altar steps
The way a man in Galilee

Came down the hill to feed
Five thousand with two fish
And five barley loaves.

He holds the thin unleavened host,
No larger than a coin,
Places it on outstretched hand or tongue.

'The body of Christ.' 'Amen.'
'The body of Christ.' 'Amen.'
The words echo their mantra,

Faith twinned with adoration.
He balances the miracles,
Ponders which is harder to believe.

PATEN

About the same age as the boy
       With barley loaves and fish,
The acolyte moves beside the priest,
       Matches him step for step
Along the sanctuary rails,

Holds the paten level under
       Pious chins, notes
That girls don't have an Adam's apple
       (Something to do with Eden,
With earning 'your bread by the sweat

Of your brow'), daydreams about a hill
       In Galilee, sees
Himself collect the scraps left
       Over by five thousand
Men, twelve hamper baskets full.

MONSTRANCE

The monstrance burns on the altar,
        Flames bursting out like rays of sun,
A gold inferno surrounding the host,
The round host at the centre, white
        As a full moon on a cloudless night,
Stars flickering like attendant candles.

And like the ancient sun and moon
        It invites adoration. Entering and leaving,
The faithful genuflect, worship on both knees
As their ancestors fell prostrate before their gods,
        Prayed and chanted fervent as the congregation's
Tribal hymns: 'Adoro Te', 'Tantum Ergo',

Hymns I knew by heart and sang with heart
        Holding hands I loved, plugged in
To the power points of belief. Today,
I dropped into a church like visiting
        A friend who might, or not, remember me.
Again, a monstrance flamed on the high altar,

Radiant as the sun. The white moon
        At the centre looked at me with its cyclops' eye,
Trained its closed circuit camera on my soul.
The candles on both sides winked recognition.
        I missed the charge from hands I used to hold
And, leaving, genuflected on both knees.

SANCTUARY LAMP

Sanctuary speaks 'hunchback', 'bells',
    Esmeralda's cup of water
Outside Notre Dame,
    Laughton's cyclops' eye
Defining pain.

Inside parochial altar rails
    This lamp pulses, glows,
Points to golden eagles
    On the tabernacle door,
Announces God's 'at home'.

It hypnotises,
    Holds the gaze, compelling
As a comet's tail,
    Draws like some trapped miner's lamp
Tunnelling towards light.

The long wick flickers; flame floats
    On sanctuary oil.
The lamp hangs from a marble wall,
    A two thousand year vintage
Glass of wine.

The lady with a shopping bag
    Genuflects, faces the rain,
Climbs the staircase to her flat,
    Switches on the electric light,
Sets his place for tea.

THURIBLE

Charcoal came in boxes, each piece
Round as a communion host
But black, a cross gouged at its centre.
We held it in a tiny tongs

Above the taper's flame, fanned
The glow like crouching cavemen
Finding fire, our contribution
Towards some molten dawn, then placed it

In the thurible's deep cradle,
Swung it gently to keep the blush
Alive. The clank and jangle of the chains
Echoed some heavenly drawbridge

As the celebrant spooned incense
From the silver boat. A slight sizzle
And then the aromatic cloud
Searching for corners of the soul.

Incense was a wise man's gift
Brought to another cradle lined
With straw. A whiff evokes the solemn
Priests in solemn cloth-of-gold,

'Clothed in the sun', or, dressed in black
Vestments and cope, blessing coffins
Surrounded by black candles, poised
On trestles before the altar.

At funerals, the boat assumed
Its role as 'craft of Christ', the spoon
A paddle to row across Jordan.
Like that morning when six young men

In black berets shouldered the coffin.
The papers carried photos of the crowds,
The horse-drawn hearse, strangers,
Me swinging a thurible.

CANDLES

The feet of the Madonna are warmed
    With penny candles: daisies
In a humming meadow, little tongues
    Panting with petition and praise.

On the high altar, candelabra
    Spread their peacock tails.
Candles slink, slim and graceful
    Dancers on a Goldwyn stairwell.

Mass candles are beeswax rich,
    Reminders of the catacombs,
Illuminating gospel and epistle
    With their flickering splinters of sun.

Around the coffin, six stand
    Tall as sentinels. Not white
But dripping black tears,
    Their flame burns just as bright.

TAPER

In white lace surplice and red
Soutane, the acolyte glides
From candle to candle waving
His taper, his wand of light.
Its hot kiss is a spark
From some dead star, a shard
Of Genesis echoing
Creation's, ' Let there be light.'

Like a lustral Rembrandt
Illuminating souls,
Its white tongue dances, spreads
The Pentecostal gossip
Of its flame, signals
'Curtain up' on celebration,
Burns until the death
Of innocence or praise.

EXTINGUISHER

Deft as a flyfisher,
The acolyte holds
The long cane handle
That reaches stars

And the tallest candles.
This wand brings darkness,
Dowses liturgies,
Snuffs the oxygen

On celebration, sacrifice.
Sudden as sunset,
It drops. But the taper
In its cap (that thin

White feather, that plume
Of flame) offers hope
Of light, of dawn,
Of resurrection.

AMICE

You cannot see the amice,
The rectangular linen cloth
Worn around neck and shoulders
To protect the outer vestments.

'A little hood', 'a cap'
Once worn on the head,
The rubric still insists it touches
The priest's head before wearing.

You cannot see the amice,
Now hidden by the alb for neatness.
And such a little thing
To take on faith.

ALB

The long white linen tunic
Is gathered by a cincture at the waist.
Tunica talaris, with its echo of toil,
The Greco-Roman garment of everyday use.

They wore it scattering seed in spring,
Digging for fruits of the earth,
Selling daily bread in the marketplace,
Fishing on lakes like Galilee,
On hillsides, watching sheep,
Climbing through windows in the dark.

An acolyte rings the sacristy bell,
Precedes the priest to the altar,
The priest tall in his flowing alb,
Dressed for the daily chores:

His words falling on good and stony ground,
His digging deep for treasure in heaven,
His breaking of bread on the altar,
His mission of fishing for men,
His promise of feeding the lambs, the sheep,
His ritual after the thief in the night.

At the foot of the cross, soldiers
Cast lots for a tunic like this.
The lucky one brought it home,
Tried to wash away the blood.

MANIPLE

Cut from the same material
As chasuble and stole,
The maniple dangles
From the priest's left arm.

Its history travels the roads
To ancient Rome, a cloth
To dry the moisture from the face
And wipe the mouth at meals.

No longer functional,
It ornaments the liturgy of food:
The breaking of bread at the altar,
The drinking of communion wine.

Good Friday is the day
Without a Eucharistic meal
And so the dark day in the year
When the maniple is not worn.

The word also referred
To Roman legions,
Their subdivisions of sixty
Or a hundred and twenty souls,

Souls that would understand
When maniples are not worn,
Souls haunted by the echo of nails
From Golgotha to the Appian Way.

STOLE

The cross-my-heart vestment
Descended from imperial pomp,
Worn by priests of the God
Who supplanted the gods,

Worn when water trickles
Down the down of babies' heads
In stone and marble fonts
Cascading ritual,

Worn before high altars
When rings are interchanged
And, down from higher windows,
Sunshine solders loves,

Worn in cavernous confessionals
Where secrets worm the dark,
Where pawned light is redeemed
By the bright coins of remorse.

And, kneeling by death-beds, curates
Drape silk stoles ('the reins of God')
Around their necks: advocates
Before the highest court.

CINCTURE

The cincture hung longer in lent,
Tucked the alb tighter in at the waist,
But mostly symbolised
A different kind of fast,

A teeth-on-edge abstinence,
A girdle to gird up the loins
Against some sin without a name,
Some honeyed temptation,

A hissing evil coiled
From the electric prods
Of pulpit, ambo, altar;
Writhing at the high-voltage rods

Of words painting eternal flames,
The Virgin Mother's prayer,
Sermons plugged into the mains
Of innocence betrayed.

Betrayal like the apostle
Slinking off early from Da Vinci's
Meal, signalling to soldiers
With his eponymous kiss.

Thirty pieces of silver
Were black stars in his sky
When loosening his cincture,
Searching for a tree.

CHASUBLE

They called it 'snail shell',
'Little house'.
The Saville Row cut of vestments,
An everyday garment
Of Athens and ancient Rome.
Fitting all sizes
From El Greco saints to Friar Tucks,
Its conical shape unrolls
(A halo hole for the head)
Like wallpaper,
Dry waterfalls,
Down front and back,
Dovetails towards the heel
In a liturgy of peace.

Chasubles are chameleon,
Blend with feast days,
The seasons of the soul:
Nature's green,
White for virgins, wise and unwise,
Red for the flood of martyrs' blood,
Penitential purple,
Always black for requiems,
The shadows of the dead.

My favourite was cloth-of-gold,
The square-cut gold for glory
On the calendar's golden days,
Heavy as armour,
Fashioned like d'Artagnan's
And his misnomered musketeers'.
Our matinee heroes
Swashbuckled for justice,
Championed the weak and beautiful,
Then sat down by the final reel
Carousing in some inn:
'All for one and one for all!'
Sharing bread and flagons of fine wine.

Not so unlike disciples at Emmaus:
'Where two or three are gathered in my name . . .'
Not so unlike the celebrant
With a cross embroidered on his back.

COPE

Massive as conscience,
They draped the shoulders
Of kings and prelates,
Ancient warlords.
Icarus might have worn one
Darkening the sun.

The acolytes walk in twos
Leading the candlelit
Procession to evening benediction.
Behind them, the priest in his white cope
Spread like the feathers
Of a mother hen sheltering her brood.

At solemn requiems,
The copious cope is black.
The celebrant circles the coffin,
Sprinkles water, swings the thurible.
Six black candles
Catch a glint of raven.

White copes celebrate
With peacock pride;
Wings flutter like doves.
Cavernous black diminish
To vampire bats, fly into the bright
Hole in the sky that we call 'moon'.

BIRETTA

Morning on morning, the *déjà vu*
Of acolyte and priest making brief
Procession between sacristy and altar:

The acolyte in surplice and soutane,
        The priest in vestments of the day
Capped with black biretta.

He wore it reverentially again
        At evening Benediction.
These were gentle services

When we could imagine the three-
        Cornered biretta as wafers
Crowning trifle or ice cream.

But such day dreams were clouded
        By preachers bounding the pulpit steps
On yet another fierce campaign

For the church too militant. We cowered
        As if behind siege walls under attack
By some Cromwell or foreign prince

When words were hurled like molten
        Cannon balls, and the biretta's
Corners were shark fins off the reef.

INTROIT

'Introibo ad altare Dei,
Ad Deum Qui laetificat juventutem meam.'

'I will go unto the altar of God,
To God Who gives joy to my youth.'

The stone steps to the church are smoother now,
The stone steps slippery with Limerick rain.

This was our theatre and concert hall,
Art gallery and, some would say, museum.

First steps to the thrill of pageantry,
Gazing at the monstrance, cope, the cloth-of-gold,

Dazzled by the multi-coloured light
Of stained-glass windows, their jig-saw saints.

The pieta was not Carrara marble
But still echoed that Michelangelo.

The extracts from epistle and gospel
Knitted to our 'Golden Treasury',

And 'Hamlet' and 'King Lear' had competition
From the drama of crib and crucifix,

Our priest actors no less theatrical
In seasonal vestments. Again, all male.

A shy soprano in the gallery
Could dream 'La Traviata' at The Met.

All this and the comfort of belief.
Youth gifted with the joy of possibility

Beckoning to feet on two stone steps
Slippery with rain and holy water.

KYRIE

For the times we did not gasp in awe
At sparrows on a twig,
Kyrie eleison.

For not preserving love at the right temperature,
Not checking the humidity,
Kyrie eleison.

For taking sides in the struggle
Between mongoose and snake,
Kyrie eleison.

For burying the talent in a napkin
Then not being able to find the spot,
Kyrie eleison.

For not walking on water when all
It needed was the buoyancy of faith,
Kyrie eleison.

For thinking to forget the dead
Was to let them rest in peace,
Kyrie eleison.

For presuming the unrepentant thief
Did not enter paradise,
Kyrie eleison.

For imagining, because you don't have
A website, perhaps you don't exist,
Kyrie eleison.

GLORIA

For the hand that scattered stars
Like dice in a casino,
Gloria.

For the fireballs bowled,
Skittling ninepins in the sky,
Gloria.

For everything between sea floor
And wren on the eagle's back,
Gloria.

Especially the child in the maternity ward,
Its tear anointing the cycle,
Gloria.

For the mother cradling down the steps
A gift from heaven to earth,
Gloria.

For poppies and cowslips,
The butterfly wings in her meadow,
Gloria.

For the daisy chain moments
Linking her youth with age,
Gloria.

For the hand that guides her back the steps
To that place before the tear,
Gloria.

To the force behind the fireball, stars,
The butterfly and daisy,
Gloria in excelsis.

EPISTLE

Today, he would be clocking up air miles,
Checking in at Athens, Corinth, Ephesus
Or Rome, the good news in his jetstream,
Block capital letters across the sky.

Saul of Tarsus who watched the witnesses'
Piled clothes, like schoolboys in a playground fight,
While Stephen fell under the comet cluster,
The zealous shower of meteoric stones.

Ardent Saul knocked down from his horse
And entering the language at Damascus.
New man Paul, his soul refurbished, proving
Quill and papyrus are mightier than the sword.

Two thousand years down the road, his website
Would be flooded, 'Better to marry than to burn'
Competing with 'Though I speak with the tongue
Of angels and have not charity,

I am as sounding brass or a tinkling
Cymbal' for the all-time greatest hit.

GOSPEL

I keep it with his letters,
My father's Testament:
Gospels, Epistles, Acts.
The War Office's complimentary copy
With its message of love
And eternal life.
'Presented': Algiers, North Africa,
Wednesday 7th July 1943.

The first page has his name
Inked with a broad-nibbed pen:
A swan's-neck capital 'G',
The 'k' and 'y' familiar,
The dot racing before the 'i'
Identical to mine.

For 'Home Address' he gives
The George Hotel.
He lists his wife 'Nearest of Kin',
Also c/o The Royal George Hotel,
Where they had met,
Where she still worked,
Where, every morning, she prayed
For a card or letter
With a swan's neck capital 'G',
The censor's 'imprimatur' stamp.

The last page is a note
From Chief of Chaplains, headed
'Do you know your chaplain?'
He got to know him very well,
Better with each amputation,
Dictating letters with the soldier's promise,
'I'll be back.'

After the letters, his testament of love,
They sent her his New Testament.
Later, the photograph
Of the mound of fresh Italian earth,
The wooden cross.

CREDO

When to use capitals was easy,
Even Duggan understood:
'Starting a sentence, proper names'
(Reeling off a rehearsed litany –
'Jack, Marie, Dublin, London,
Liffey, Thames, Valparaiso'),
'"I" when referring to yourself.'
He swelled his stomach to a capital 'O',
Pronounced the Everest of rules:
'And always a capital "G" for God.'

Of course, by 'God' he meant our god,
The one born in a stable every Christmas,
Warmed by the breath of ox and cow
While Joseph was collecting wood,
The carpenter nailed to a Roman cross
Then rising from the coldest bed.
Tried in fires degrees beyond
The heat of ox and cow, belief
Evaporated by degrees.
Despite the rules, my Judas pen
Began to hesitate at 'g'.

OFFERTORY

The picture-postcard children
    Balance cut-glass cruets
And full ciborium,
    Lead a small procession
Towards the sanctuary steps.

Behind them, two adults
    With their wicker collection trays,
Notes and coins, a widow's mite
    In place of bread,
A vintage flagon of red wine.

Little here to hint at lambs' blood
    Drenching altar cloths,
At Isaac shouldering dry wood
    To a place of sacrifice,
At Abraham binding his only son.

The organist pulls out the stops,
    Is heavy on the pedals, keys,
As if some fervent score or hymn
    Could drown that distant thunder roll,
That *furioso* hammering of nails.

LAVABO

At Cana's wedding feast,
Mary's son turned water into wine.

When Pilate tried
As best he could
To get in on the magic act,

Rinsing guilty fingers
Turned water into blood.

PREFACE

A moment still as sunset
On a white sand beach,
Quiet as tip-toeing stars
Across the velvet sky.

A hold-your-breath
Edge of jungle moment
Downwind of bird,
Big cat and butterfly.

A carpet-cushioned pause
Too soft for echoes.
If any word were whispered now,
It would insist,

'Take off your shoes.
You walk on holy ground.'

SANCTUS

Incense rose like scented cloud
And the sanctuary steps were white
As snow on Clare's December hills.
Kneeling in whiter surplice
And red soutane, I fingered
The familiar bell, delighting
As the four brass tongues sang
'*Sanctus. Sanctus. Sanctus.*'

Delighting now in bluebells
Mirroring the sky, in robins
Flickering on a garden fence,
Ladybirds abseiling dandelions,
A gladiator spider flinging his net,
The surprise of a salmon's sickle leap,
My acolyte fingers itch
For the sanctus bell's three fervent chimes.

CONSECRATION

Cana's miracle can't hold
A beeswax candle up to this.
Water into wine may be explained
By some illusionist on prime-time television

But here, a latter-day Melchisedech,
Dressed in ceremonial chasuble,
Throws no smoke screen, indulges
In no practised sleight of hand.

Here, nobody deceives the eye,
Simply the formulaic words
'This is my body. This my blood,'
Pronounced above the host, the altar wine.

A bell tinkles. A genuflection.
No outburst of applause, no cheers
For the magician centre-stage.
Just heads now bowed in adoration.

The difference invisible except to faith,
That complicated choosing to believe,
The plunge, the headlong dive colluding
In a mystery of change.

Every consecration bell vibrates
Its question mark. And knees respond.
Most with genuflections, certain, firm.
A few knee-jerk reactions.

PATER NOSTER

We know god through analogy,
The theologians say.
Like us but utterly other.

I never said, '*Abba*, Father.'
He died too young.
But I knew my grandfather,

His dawn solo each morning,
His rat-tat-tat-tat on the bedroom door
Signalling my mother's resurrection,

His stories by the winter fire
Creating a shiver
Despite the blue-flame coals

And, mostly, jumping
On the bar of his bike
For the spin to his Corbally plot

Where blackbirds' lyrics were sweeter
Than the singing from any golden bough
Of Yeats' Byzantium,

Where he dug potato drills
While I played in the sun
And in his shadow.

Fathers, problematic.
But God the grandfather
I can easily understand.

I would jump up on the bar
Of his old Raleigh any day
And listen to his stories

While he pedalled all the way
To an eternal paradise
That I already know by analogy.

THE KISS OF PEACE

We turn from sacrificial altars,
Meet the eye of someone just like us,
Discover 'Who is my neighbour?'.

Too shy for kissing, we just shake hands,
Instinctively decode each grip:
The firm, the soft, the fractionally prolonged.

The instant brothersisterhood is not friendship
But, like the Sistine god and Adam,
Fingers spark currents between heaven and earth.

About the kissing, perhaps it is the shadow
Cast from Da Vinci's 'Last Supper' and falling
On Gethsemane's gate, the Judas kiss.

Now shadows lift like cloud, like purple veils
Revealing statues after Holy Week,
Revealing smiles. There is sanctity in a smile.

AGNUS DEI

Lamb of God who carried
Your bindle of hammer, nails and crown of thorns,
    Have mercy on us.

Lamb of God who gifts
A springtime resurrection of flowers and lambs,
    Have mercy on us.

Lamb of God who understands
That the lion can lie down with the lamb,
    Grant us peace.

COMMUNION

This desert has no scorpion, no snakes.
The thin procession moves on up the centre
Aisle and down the sides, tapering
To an angel's wing. Its pace is reverential,

Slow. Gathering manna, queueing
At the celestial snack bar, heads
Are bowed, hands joined. The organ hums, lips move
To hymns with tried and trusted DNA:

'Panis Angelicus', 'Soul of My Saviour',
The belt and braces repertoire of praise.
The priest opens the tabernacle door,
Reaches for the ciborium, descends

The sanctuary steps as if sandalled
In Galilee. Dispensing hosts like medicine,
He places one on outstretched hands, on every
Famished tongue. Except the scattered

Few remaining in their seats: perhaps
Some anorexic soul, Tobias mothers
Wrestling with the pill, a youth who looks
Up at the host but cannot say 'Amen',

The old man in the corner at the back
Who shed snake years recalling that May
Morning when the nuns' miraculous
Powder changed water into lemonade.

'ITE, MISSA EST'

'Go, mass has ended.'
       'Thanks be to God.'
This is when the congregation
       Scatters, the molecules disperse,
Planets zooming out the sunlit doors,
       Returning to their orbits,
Caught between worlds, momentarily.

Down to earth, some brush dust
       From the knees of Sunday best,
Check the crease is still in place
       On trousers they will wear
Holding hands along the river bank,
       Searching for the faltering word,
Jealous of a practised liturgy.

Families walk home. Children
       Wash and dry their hands
Like priests at the 'lavabo'.
       Someone assumes the busy role
Of Bethany's Martha.
       These everyday apostles
Could pose for Leonardo.

They praise the weather, chat,
       Quoting morning papers as gospel,
Swap cherished credos of opinion.
       The table is an altar without sacrifice
As they pass bowls of meat, potatoes, veg,
       Clink glasses in mock toasts.
After dessert, the kids rush out to play.

ALL SOULS' DAY

On All Souls' Day,
We left the galaxy
Of spinning tops

To kneel on cool cathedral stone
Picking purgatory's locks
With pins of prayer.

We went for broke,
Aiming for the plenaries
With total faith,

Visualising flighted souls
Dart for the doubles
On heaven's door.

Then back to the world
Of bright chalked planets
Orbiting wet streets.

THE ADVENT CALENDAR

In the caves of deep midwinter country,
    Something rattles its chains, claws its way up
For air, leaps the bonfire in the wood
    Or dresses in druidic robes to walk
In slow procession around sacred stones.

We replicate the rattle, opening,
    Day by day, the windows of the advent
Calendar, peeping at the star,
    Overhearing Gabriel whisper
Secrets in the virgin Mary's ear.

Memories collide. Following
    The star's trajectory, it came to rest
Above that warm stable in Bethlehem
    The same midnight that Santa's reindeer
Pranced above our chimney, dropping gifts,

A midnight like the time I lay awake
    Peeping through an eyelid as my mother
Tied the bulging stocking to my bed,
    The night I lost belief in Father Christmas,
Transferred the total balance of my faith

To her account, a faith and love cocktail
That I still stir, that still stirs me, that helps
Explain a cap-gun and a cowboy hat
    Left by a crib two thousand years ago,
A box of myrrh left on my bed last night.

A COWBOY SUIT FOR CHRISTMAS

We believed in Father Christmas
As sure as we believed in God.
Both were loving, generous and just.
And they co-operated, Santa leaving presents
By our beds on God's birthday.
A neat arrangement that.

The frost of Christmas mornings energised:
Opening presents, mass, breakfast then play.
Indoors, we read the annuals
Or played with draughts, lead soldiers.
Outside, the streets were Tombstone for the day,
Dodge City, Kansas, Abilene.

Cap-guns and plastic rifles
Transformed us into sheriffs, desperadoes
And every critter in between
That ever rode the West.
The chief in feathered head-dress was Geronimo;
Young Eagle held a rubber tomahawk.

We all admired each other's toys,
Swapped between high noon shoot-outs
Won by the fastest gun alive.
The corner shop sold caps, a penny a roll,
Supplied us with imaginary bullets
Until called in for dinner at one o'clock.

Perhaps at six, maybe as old as seven,
I noticed Father Christmas brought Dillon
The best guns, double holsters, cowboy suits.
Dillon with the rich aunt in New York.
Easier to disbelieve in Santa
Than think he was unfair. Again, like God.

EPIPHANY

The show was 'Follow the Star'.
There and back
I held her hand, two worlds

Touching at fingerends,
Footprints
Pressing seals of love

On a crisp December page.
The moon played hide-
And-seek behind the clouds.

No shepherds woke, no angel
Plucked a single note,
But the white field

Spread like linen
Across the altar of night.
The sycamore was a Christmas tree

And between its branches
Fairy lights winked
In the distant town

That tonight was Bethlehem.
Her breath was incense
From a winter flower.

I felt a starpulse in my hand
And knew the sun would never melt
Those footprints in the snow.

THE COLOUR OF LENT

Lent meant six weeks without sweets
To ease the suffering of Christ,
Forty days of self-denial,
Of parents gasping for a fag,
Grandfathers chewing on briar pipes
Like infants with empty bottles.

The liturgy chose well with purple,
Not quite black and certainly not white,
A lukewarm colour tepid between death
And resurrection. Purple vestments,
Purple clouds, the city cold under
The purple shadow of its wing,

Waiting, enduring, knowing the sojourn
Must end, taking clues from daffodils,
Sparrows embroidering the sky,
A hint of buds detonating
Between cobbles, any crumb of manna
In the wilderness of anticipation.

And then the eastering world,
The ghost drapes lifted in the church
From crucifix and statue, my squirrel
Hoard of sweets retrieved from the wardrobe,
Christy Ryan loosening his belt,
The purple sky erased and painted blue.

THE BAD THIEF

Sometimes, through kindness, soldiers flogged men
Half to death before hammering in the nails,
The shock and loss of blood subtracting
From the time it took a man to die.

They showed a further kindness to the man
Called 'The Bad Thief', breaking both his legs.
His lungs collapsed, inducing a dry drowning.
The nails denied him floundering relief.

Perhaps the wood smelt like his infant cot.
Perhaps he was again that child too hurt
For tears. Perhaps they placed his body
In his mother's arms. The gospels do not say.

HER CROWN OF THORNS

After the deposition from the cross,
She held her son again
Like she had held Him as a child,
Tried to kiss better
His hands and feet and side,
Removed the thorns
With practised tenderness
As she had done when He
Came crying home from play.
Thorns were her receivers.
Tuned in to His wave-band.
She placed the crown,
Like one might place a pillow,
Underneath her head.

EUCALYPTUS

In the shadow of the wedgetail's
Wing, the bush fire rages
Like a red-faced lout tormenting
Dingos, rabbits, wallabies;

Snapping dragonflies,
Frying mulga snakes
Like eels. And no zig-zagging
Between Ghost Gum, Ironback

And Southern Blue. Just
Survival of the lucky
Till a stitch in the side slows
The fierce inferno down,

A tug on the hamstring sees
It pull up short: spent,
Quenched, collapsing into dust.
Then eggshell silence

And the wait for wind to rake the ashes
From hell's grate. But before
The buzz of flies and first canaries
Test the air, seeds peck

At their casings, hatch underground
Like tiny chicks believing
In the warmth of resurrection.
Sudden shoots easter,

Dream of saplings, trees;
Understand why this is where
The phoenix breaks his flight
To Heliopolis and the altar of the sun.

PARACLETE

Trapped at Sunday mass, the pigeon
Circled, fluttered and flapped above
The serried, reverential heads.

A fallible compass, its beak
Crashed into pillar and beam, every
Fluted arch. A failure too

As diamond, not cutting it
With stained-glass windows of apostles,
Hosts of technicolour saints.

Escaping on a shaft of light,
He soared towards the steeple, settled
On the gold archangel's spear,

Scanned the street for upper rooms:
Venues for a mighty wind,
For words smithied in tongues of fire.

MYSTERIES
(In memory of my mother)

I

If surprise is the measure
Of ignorance, she was
Ignorant indeed when
Rushed to the basin by morning
Sickness. Not a flutter
Of an angel's wing. Not
A tickle of a word in her ear.
Just hormonal tears,
A gradual ballooning the same
As before and a craving for ice cream.

II

In a winter of war, her
Step was light to his mother's door,
Casting footprints in plaster-
Of-Paris snow. Making her
Guess the secret, she felt
Her stomach like fingers telling
Braille: 'Call him after
His father.' She half
Surmised a painful
Premonition of exchange.

III

There was no manger,
No shepherds, no star,
No ox, no cow,
No donkey, camel, no
Coming from afar
Wise men bearing
Gifts. It was summer
And again she was the door
To life. Proud as Mary, she was
Almost as confused.

IV

The celebrant stood
In cloth-of-gold. The wine-filled
Chalice sparkled on the altar
Stone. A celestial choir
Released the liturgy's
Latinate praise and, through
The stained-glass apostle's
Eye, a shaft of sunlight
Shone on the trinity
Of mother, daughter, son.

V

Six o'clock; the angelus
Signalling tea. Missing
Again. No sign. She
Called into the street,
Asked neighbours, friends.
In the cathedral grounds,
Picking chestnuts, he
Had nothing clever to say;
No excuses, like doing
Something for his dad.

VI

Time's lips came early, slobbering
A Judas kiss on the young blush
Of her happiness. Holding
Hands over tea in the room overlooking
The garden, the minutes limped
Like hours listening to his talk
Of war, his regiment, his duty
Honour-bound. She drank
And read the storm of tea leaves gathering
In the bottom of her chalice.

VII

By the pillar where they knelt
Each Sunday, she opened
The letter again. The words
Unmade flesh, their gangrene
Smell cancelling incense,
Their echo of grenades
And the surgical sawing of limbs
Deafening the Sanctus, each
Syllable a thong of the lash
Flaying her naked heart.

VIII

Taking her coat with the purple lining,
She walked along the riverbank.
By a whitethorn bush, she read
The telegram, memorised
'Multiple wounds'. Rain
Spat on the paper. Blind with grief,
She couldn't tell which promise
Taunted, slapped her face: 'Nothing
Can separate us!' 'Love
Conquers all!' 'I'll be back!'

IX

His rosary was sent
With his effects, its tiny
Cross polished with use. She
Kept it in her bag, carried
It everywhere in the town where
All roads led to Calvary.
Women especially
Recognised her grief, guessed
That each night her face stained the pillow
Like Veronica's veil.

X

No nails. No spear. No
Blood and water from her side.
No thieves, but holding in each hand
A child whose paradise was
To be with her. So not forsaken,
Quite. And thirst? There was the memory
Of love, though memory could not rain
On her parched body, her deserted soul.
And always she heard the roll of dice
Cast for life's seamless robe.

XI

His knuckle tattoo on the bedroom
Door 'would wake the dead', drumming
Her from dreams to classroom, her
Wide eyes pivoting like daisies
Towards the sun. Later, the rat-
Tat-tat woke his widowed
Child to wake in turn her children
From the dream. She watched their petals
Open to light, aware of her own
Eyelids rolling back like stone.

XII

'Back in a minute,' the promise
Rang, testing relativity.
Then, after the visit, a little
Treat: the reward for patience and faith.
Perhaps a boyfriend's gold-wrapped
Toffee or an apple from an aunt
On the hill. The wait was longest when the train
Pulled out from Platform 2
And she waved to the children clutching, in brown
Paper bags, a consolation of fruit.

XIII

A pigeon in a cardboard box,
The flame of its feathers quenched with pain.
They fed it bread and water,
Watched the impatient patient limp
Until magician time whipped
Away its bandage like a handkerchief
Of silk. Soaring to the cathedral spire,
Fanned by an evening breeze
And lit by a tapering sun,
Its recreated wings caught fire.

XIV

A silver birch is her memorial,
Blessing the plot where she was born:
A traffic triangle
Once a lodge, her mother's home
Where she had spread anticipating
Thighs, her birthing estuary,
And felt life swim on the ebbing tide
Of blood. Above the highest
Arrowhead leaves, a white veil of cloud ,
A blue dress of sky.

XV

'Queenie, Queenie. Who has the ball?'
Still guessing who caught the bouncing
Globe, they called her in for bed.
But the Sunday sermon pencilled
Everlasting joy.
She smiled down at her sister,
Stripped her mind to bathe in the pulpit's
Promises: 'And nobody will wake
You up for school or call you in from play
In the eternal holiday.'

THE CATHEDRAL OF THE PINES

(Rindge, New Hampshire)

Inside the Bell Tower, the bird sets
On the Tree of Life, artificial
As beaten gold on a golden bough.

Sipping from the fountain, her song is universal,
Mute. Every creed supplies its score,
Lyrics with no wish to proselytise.

And the tree is nurtured by the Waters of Life,
Its vestments the colour of the season.
'The leaves of the tree were for the healing of nations.'

The Knoll is high as the vertigo mount
Where scandalous Satan tempted Christ,
Offering him the world if he would jump.

Nobody jumps here. Christian, Muslim,
Hindu, Jew . . . worship at this altar.
On a clear day, you can touch the floor of heaven.

The morning sun unveils the patterns stitched on grass;
Dew rises like incense. The setting sun
Burns like a monstrance's twenty-four carat rays.

Perched on her pine stall, a cantor cardinal
Sings to men, women and children of the world,
Her 'Gloria' strictly non-denominational.

THE MIRACLE WORKER

It used to be so simple. You could feed
A curious five thousand with five barley loaves
And two fishes, make a neat symbolic point
And everyone was grateful. Now you get
The vegans up in arms and food fads
Sold on wheat and rye: the allergy brigade.
Magic a draught of fishes and all hell
Breaks loose about fishery allocations
And net specifications, menageries
Of 'ations as if the sea can be sliced like cake.
Rebuke the gale and lullaby the waves.
What then? Deflated surfers get the sulks,
And forecasters blame you for all their howlers.
Walk on water and you take the flak
For every drowning since old Noah's flood.
Cure a blind man with your spittle and he serves
Writs for more infections than the judge
Can spell, then claims redress for trauma
Occasioned by the ugliness all 'round.
For pity, make ten lepers clean. One
Might thank you, but the nine? The nine resent
The crowd they work with now, the office chores
And forty-hour-a-week assembly line:
Nostalgia for the bell and begging bowl.
Invite a cripple to take up his bed
And doctors blast a blunderbuss of suits,
Infest with threats, send 'psychosomatic'
Buzzing on gadfly wings. Take the next step:
Dare raise some woman's brother from the dead,
So dead that when you roll the stone 'he stinketh',
And priests proclaim you a blasphemer,
Master of the necromantic arts,
Decree that graves be shovelled six feet deep.
Tortured with texts and questions, interminably
Racked between committees and tribunals,
The poor man sits bemused, addled in extremis,
Conscious only of a blinding light
And that strange sentence: 'Lazarus, come forth!'
It gets to you. I have this premonition
Of Roman sadists crucifying some guy.
And what alarm, outcry? Friends of the Earth
With flasks and banners voicing concern about trees.

L'ASCENSEUR DES SABRES

A mongrel pup is curious at the scent
Of blood. Cameras click, people cheer.
A Hindu youth descends the ladder of swords.

Beggar, tourist, priest, focus on feet
That survive the blades of ninety-nine machetes:
Feet lacerated, crimson in their holy wounds.

His journey echoes mediaeval pilgrims,
Sanctifies the blades like ancient shoes
On their sojourn from shrine to blessed shrine,

The same quest as smooth-skinned Jacob dreaming
Angels shinning the ladder wedged
Between earth and the blue floor of heaven,

The same impulse as Sun Dance warriors
Hooked delirious in tents until
The tear of skin, the windfall apple drop.

Like Bernini's marble Teresa,
The boy's face glows, radiates his ecstasy
Of pain. And 'round his feet, bluebottles buzz,

Cousins to the dark low cloud of flies
That plagued the feet nailed to a Roman cross,
A cross without a ladder to climb down.

SENEX

White as a ghost, the almost ghost
Lies between linen sheets.
The family haunt his bedside.
Like mothers mistaking

The grimace of wind for a smile,
They read tranquillity
On papyrus skin
Though his skull is a hollow

Cathedral echoing
With sermons on hell fire,
Furnaced with words that froze
His blood before thought

Rode up in shining armour
And levelled its lance at the mouth
Of his dragon's cave. His lips
Are silent now,

Too tired to whisper
That the dragon has revived.
And nobody sees his mind
Curve back to childhood

Like the graph of his bent spine.
Silence amplifies
The pain of sulphur
Suffocating skin,

The tide of molten lava
Lapping round his feet,
The red coals pulsing
In the sockets of his eyes.

EN ROUTE TO PARADISE

I still remember when the body burst,
Leaking from its coffin in the church's
Mortuary, soaking the pall and dripping
Down the trestles like tears. Anxious

To reassure, the priest enthused on reaping
What we sow, was eloquent on the sleep
Of all the just, the good fight fought and won,
The best of shepherds caring for his sheep.

He reached to pull the ripest clichés down,
Plucked berries from the bush of consolation.
No reference to the fruit that Adam ate,
No syllable on hell's eternal flame

As sesames of prayer unlocked the gates
Of heaven. His words were fluttering flowers of faith.
But I remember most the smell of death.
Yes, I remember most the smell of death.

THE PARISH BELL

Her highway code on the road
To heaven, its single ring
Announced the morning mass
And evening benediction.

The double toll was cue
For shops to pull the blinds
And passers-by to stand
In reverent silence,

To bless themselves, half prayer
Half superstition,
As Thompson's matching mares
(Shadows of apocalypse)

Drew the hearse past school,
Dancehall and hospital,
Then whinnied to a halt
At the cemetery gate.

The three threes and a nine
Scored 'Angelus ad virginem'
As she dropped stitches and kitchen
Chores to join in prayer

With the fieldworkers of Millet's
Fading print. Her own
Fading removed her
To a hospital ward

Out of earshot of the parish
Bell. Between starched sheets,
She woke to its remembered
Invitation. I promised

I would take her coat
From its nail behind the door
And walk with her to church,
Hold her hand against the hill.

EVICTION

Here no thud of wrecking ball,
No burning thatch, no bailiff
Parroting his master's voice,
No soldiers with fixed bayonets
Keen to make a point.

This eviction was discreet,
The statue of the Virgin
Lowered from its plinth,
Trundled down the centre aisle
And winched aboard the truck
Like cattle swung and slung
Onto an island ferry.
Hardly an assumption.

As if consigned to a retirement home,
They said that she was earmarked for some grotto.

The statue stood at six feet four,
Her dress pure white,
The flowing sash sky blue,
A golden rose on each bare foot
And, dangling by her side,
The golden rosary that sinners climbed,
Their ladder into heaven.

Her fingers were not bowered in prayer;
The mediatrix's slender hands
Had broken off in transit
And, at the back, her long white dress
Was nothing like immaculate,
Seldom painted with the rest
Because she stood against the wall.

All those years we were unaware
That her back was to the wall.

PASSING ST. MICHAEL'S

I almost passed you on the street
But lingered. Something about the ancient
Door, cold stone, my fingers' instinct
For the water font, my knee intent

On reflex genuflection. Inside,
The same tiled floor and silence,
Marble pillars pointing to the
Frescoed ceiling, your book's page

Thumbed at the gospel of St. John.
Stained-glass angels filtered sun,
Trained it on the table's linen
Cloth spread out for supper. Again,

The flicker of beeswax candles,
The fragrant liturgy of flowers,
Unleavened bread and chalices
Of red wine, the resonant organ's

Serenade of wall to wall
Plain-song. Then the glow of charcoal,
Its deep slow burn, and the smell
Of incense evocative as Chanel.

ON HOLD

Apart from God and me, the church was empty:
God behind the tabernacle's golden gates,
Me kneeling on the centre aisle's back bench
Where the last-in-first-out brigade would slink
In late for Sunday mass, crouched, one knee
On their cloth caps, sprinters in their blocks.

The sanctuary lamp's red glow announced
That He was in, and then the wall-to-wall
Canned music, the far from plain plain-chant
Of cowled and cloistered monks anointing
With an ancient Latinate balm like some
Celestial call-centre putting me on hold.

When silence dropped its net, it caught me mute
As Zechariah before naming John.
Again, the resonant monastic vowels,
The plait of base and tenor notes honeyed
By faith. And my turn missed at the exchange.
Perhaps He'll call me back. He has my number.

Note on 'Mysteries'

The Joyful Mysteries of the Rosary:

The Annunciation
The Visitation
The Nativity
The Presentation in the Temple
The Finding of the Child Jesus in the Temple

The Sorrowful Mysteries of the Rosary:

The Agony in the Garden
The Scourging at the Pillar
The Crowning with Thorns
The Carrying of the Cross
The Crucifixion

The Glorious Mysteries of the Rosary:

The Resurrection
The Ascension
The Descent of the Holy Spirit on the Apostles
The Assumption of Our Lady into Heaven
The Crowning of Our Lady Queen of Heaven

Acknowledgements

Acknowledgements are due to the editors of the following magazines etc. in which some of these poems first appeared:

Acumen
Chimera
The Limerick Leader
Littoral
Magma
Microphone On
Poetry Ireland
Revival
Stony Thursday
Wasafiri